taking time for tea

diana rosen

STOREY
BOOKS

The mission of Storey Publishing is to serve our customers by publishing practical information that encourages personal independence in harmony with the environment.

Edited by Robin Catalano and Deborah Balmuth
Cover and interior design and production by Carol Jessop, Black Trout Design
Photo montages by Carol Jessop using photos by Giles Prett and Artville™; except photos on pages 2, 3, 5, 6, 10, 15, 17, 18, 21, 26, 29, and 73 by John Conte
Indexed by Nina Forrest, Looking Up Indexing Service

The information in this book is true and complete to the best of our knowledge. All recommendations are made without guarantee on the part of the author or Storey Publishing. The author and publisher disclaim any liability in connection with the use of this information. For additional information, please contact Storey Books, 210 MASS MoCA Way, North Adams, MA 01247.

Storey books are available for special premium and promotional uses and for customized editions. For further information, please call Storey's Custom Publishing Department at (800) 793-9396.

Printed in the United Kingdom by Butler & Tanner, Ltd.
10 9 8 7 6 5 4 3

Library of Congress Cataloging-in-Publication Data

Rosen, Diana
    Taking time for tea / Diana Rosen.
      p.   cm.
    ISBN 1-58017-245-8 (alk. paper)
    1. Afternoon teas. 2. Tea. 3. Menus. I. Title.
  TX736 .R67 2000
  641.5'3—dc21
                                               00-025545
                                                              CIP

ACKNOWLEDGMENTS

Thank you to the entire staff of Storey Books; you make the writer-publisher experience a pleasure.

contents

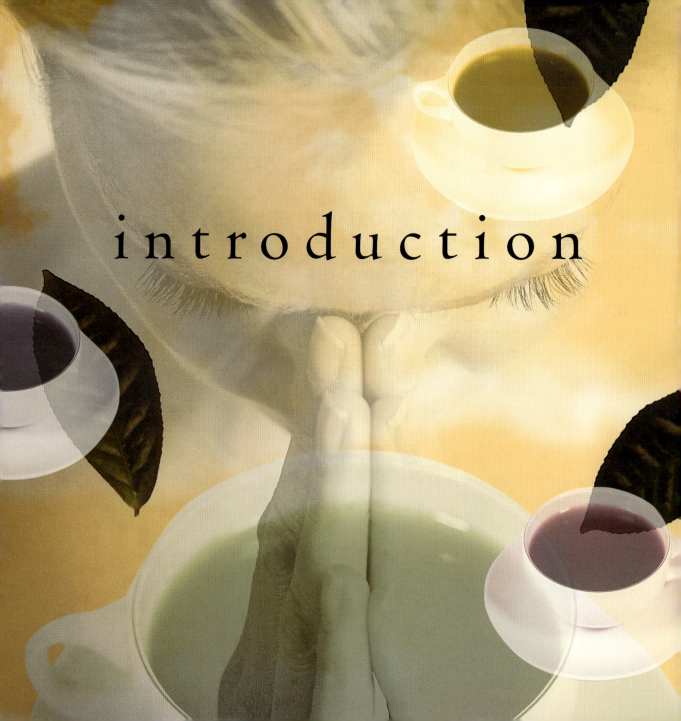

introduction

Taking a bowl of green tea in your hands and drinking it, you feel one with nature, and there is peace. This peace can be spread by offering a bowl of tea to another. I hope you will drink and share this peace with me.

— Soshitsu Sen XV, *Tea Life, Tea Mind*

what tea means to me

As the venerable fifth-generation Japanese tea master writes so elegantly, tea is a metaphor for peace. Drinking tea alone is a form of meditation, a way of releasing the cares of the day, allowing a sense of accomplishments and satisfactions to embrace us.

Drinking tea is also a form of community, with one person or many, in which common interests or goals are exchanged and the foundation of friendship is strengthened. Serving tea to strangers, to new business associates, or to government officials is a way to soften, to appease, to make calm, so that all can meet, work, and rule in some comfort and style.

Taking the time to prepare tea for others is an important bridge of communication, and carefully preparing tea for ourselves is a vital link to our deepest core.

This, then, is what tea means to me: the embrace of friendship, quiet contemplation, and the sustenance that can bring inner serenity and peace.

For more than 10 years, I have been a willing student of all the pleasures of tea. If I had only encountered my childhood black tea served in a glass, drunk over a sugar cube melting on my tongue, I would have been happy. If I had only encountered a blend of the world's best blacks silkened with milk, served with a buttery scone, I would have been delighted. If I had only sipped the exquisitely fragrant oolong served *gung fu*–style in a tiny Taiwanese clay teapot and poured into tinier cups, I would have visited nirvana. If I had only had the many taste adventures of green teas, recalled the memory of powdered tea whisked to a frothy nectar and served in a serene Japanese tearoom, that would have been enough.

But tea has given me so much more, and it continues to do so. Tea invites me to employ all my senses. The gently bubbling sound of the water kettle; the tactile pleasures of a fine porcelain vessel in which to brew the tea; the visual delight of the ballet of unfurling leaves; the fragrance, the taste — all are parts of the wonder of tea.

When we give tea the time and care it deserves, it returns to us all its infinite gifts. Each cup is a rapturous prayer no words can describe.

I am alone with the beating of my heart . . .

— Lui Chi (first emperor of the Han dynasty)

Creating a Spiritual Place for Reflections on Tea

Everyone should have a small corner in which to relax, be quiet, reflect. It could be a hobby room with all your treasured tools and projects around you. Or a flower- and wicker-furnished atrium that overlooks a garden, or a book-lined, wood-paneled room with a roaring fire all year long to accompany your thoughts.

Perhaps you find serenity lounging in your bath with tea in a gauze bag to smooth over your wet skin, or in your boudoir with a tea-scented candle or incense emitting its sweetness, some spent tea bags placed over your eyes to rest them and reduce fatigue.

Your small corner could be a barely furnished room with a singular piece of beauty: a painting, a photograph, a sculpture that cries for the touch. Serenity for you might be gazing out the kitchen window at the birds, or being outdoors by a campfire, biking in a park, or just sitting a spell on the front-porch glider.

Spending Time with You

Give yourself 10 minutes a day to visit your special space, enjoy tea and quiet, and regenerate yourself. Even in the oddest places you can savor your "tea and ten": waiting at the airport, on the airplane itself, in a hotel room. At work, you can choose a restorative cup of tea drunk in silence in the employee lounge, on the rooftop or in an outdoor area, in the boardroom, or even at your desk. (If you do it at the same time every day, coworkers will get the hint and leave you to your tea experience. Maybe they'll even do it themselves.)

Make an appointment with yourself to meditate in the manner that feels most comfortable to you. You bathe, brush your teeth, and eat — why not include meditation with a cup of tea as one of those everyday things that are essential to your health and well-being?

Meditation with a cup of tea is time to suspend thought, ease your mind and body, and rest your soul. Giving yourself 10 minutes a day with a cup of tea will go a long way toward improving your health, your happiness, and thus your life. Meditation need not be formal, religious, or intent on solving the world's — or your — problems; it is just a Sabbath from the everyday.

Make a date with yourself right now. Choose your special corner, and give yourself just 10 minutes to savor some tea and rest your mind. Who deserves this more than you?

The path to heaven passes through a teapot.

— Ancient proverb

Celebrating the Particular with Tea

Tea-making is a theme used in hundreds of artworks throughout the Orient and the Western world. Whether it's a romantic couple by a samovar, an elegant king presiding over his royal court, or a solitary person with her teacup, tea is a vital subject for art — and life.

I am in no way interested in immortality, only in the taste of tea.
— Lu T'ung, eighth-century Chinese poet

Passages and Accomplishments

The protocol in the 19th century was that a person's name should appear but three times in the local paper: at birth, marriage, and death. This is not to say that special occasions and events were not celebrated, only that most were supposed to be private. Such limited acknowledgments are not for me. I believe every accomplishment, any exceptional endeavor, all joy, and some sorrows should be shared with friends and family over a pot of tea whenever possible.

For children, it is especially important to acknowledge all the little everyday accomplishments that go toward developing a well-rounded, productive young adult. Something as simple as a special breakfast tea can send a child off with a fortitude deeper than can the nourishment of food. Whether it's learning to tie a knot, mastering multiplication tables, riding a bike, or writing that first term paper, a modest celebration of these accomplishments demonstrates your love and appreciation for this growing, evolving being: your child.

For adults, it is critical to continue these mini-celebrations, especially when we are involved in dangerous or highly competitive careers, where praise and applause are meted out sparingly, if at all. When coworkers or employees go the extra mile, sustain production above the call, do the job with spirit and enthusiasm, it's time to acknowledge, celebrate, and honor their achievements with verbal praise, written kudos, or a cordial tea break that recognizes that these are people, not just statistics.

In good times, tea is celebratory; in bad times, it is amazingly comforting. And at all times, serving tea and "the news" to your friends helps make every sorrow easier to bear, every joy more exciting to share.

Hearing the doctor's report over tea helps us adjust to the impact. Announcing plans to move, to take another job, to commemorate anniversaries of friendship and love — all seem more special when we are surrounded by friends enjoying a hot pot of tea.

A Year of Celebrations and Reflections

Tea is a way to celebrate with others and a way to meditate on our lives. Tea helps us slow down and recognize the real world, that quieter place in us all that can deflect those sounds of the outer world that distract, disturb.

Selecting tea and water consciously, using the graceful implements of tea preparation, drinking tea mindfully and purposefully: This is meditation incarnate. We become one with tea. We become one with ourselves. Tea helps us dive into our very soul.

Tea, then, is a gift from nature to humans that helps us reach out to one another, yet connect with ourselves meaningfully.

In this book I show just a few ways in which the simple combination of tea leaf and water can be the basis for celebrations and reflections all through the year. I hope these examples will inspire you to create celebrations that are uniquely yours, to honor all the days of your life — with tea. Tea is a supreme blessing, an infinite gift, not unlike the treasure of life. May it always be the conduit between friends and family as you walk through your passages of life. And may you find your peace in a bowl of tea.

Thank you for taking time for tea with me.

A TEA BLESSING
Before me peaceful
Behind me peaceful
Under me peaceful
Over me peaceful
All around me peaceful

— Traditional
Navajo blessing

Tea is drunk to forget the din of the world.

— T'ien Yiheng (eighth-century Chinese sage)

the history & lore of tea

Centuries later, we realize the truth of T'ien's observation even more. Today's world is a noisy place, packed with the sound and tension of traffic, the vibrations of electronic equipment everywhere, the cacophony of too much mindless talk.

The modern world is invasive and omnipresent. Fortunately, there is an antidote that is inexpensive and accessible and offers therapeutic benefits for us all — tea! The relaxation one derives from a cup of tea is a decidedly powerful antidote to the din of this world.

What is it about tea that both calms and energizes? To the chemist approaching a cup of tea, the beverage reveals polyphenols and catechins, which are important antioxidants that heal and revitalize. To the tea lover, a cup of hot tea is soothing and refreshing, a conduit for relaxation and a stimulant that is gradual yet long lasting.

Tea Beginnings

Originally, Buddhist monks were the most enthusiastic devotees of tea. They readily understood how drinking tea could help them stay alert during hours of meditation, yet keep them comfortable enough so that sitting in the position of prayer was not nearly such a strain.

Tea traveled with monks first in China, the birthplace of tea, then in Japan, Korea, India, Vietnam, and Indonesia and throughout the Pan-Asiatic world. Even today, some of the purest teas are still being grown much as they have for been centuries, on lands surrounding Buddhist monasteries.

Strangely enough, humanity has so far met in the tea-cup. It is the only Asiatic ceremonial which commands universal esteem.
— Okakura Kakuzo, *The Book of Tea*

Tea in Modern Times

Before the 19th century, most people drank the popular beverage of tea in the form of green tea. Because of its fragility, green tea did not arrive in London from Canton in the same sweet, grassy state in which it was sent. After several months by clipper ship, well, let's just say it tasted indelicate.

The Chinese cleverly devised a drying method to process the tea to the now-familiar black-leaf style. This wholly processed leaf lasted months, made the trip from Canton to London with ease, and earned China worldwide, centuries-long devotion to its native plant . . . and a hefty quantity of silver, too.

Blacks are still the best-selling teas throughout the world, although green teas remain most popular within China and much of the rest of Asia. Now that the health-giving properties of green tea have been substantiated by many prestigious medical studies, green tea is enjoyed by thousands more people throughout the world.

An Introduction to the Many Types

Thanks to pioneering entrepreneurs from all over the world, we have quite a selection of fine-quality teas to choose from: leaf buds processed as whites, ephemeral in color and taste but lingering on the memory; crisp, sweet greens in shapes from rolled pellets to long, elegant leaves, or a mixture of gentle buds and green leaves for taste that lasts for several infusions; oolongs of large, full leaves releasing their heavy perfume and flavor for us to savor and remember; vibrant blacks that create reddish brews in the cup, some sweet with a roundness of flavor, others clean and crisp on the tongue.

Many of these tea pleasures are available because of the opening of doors to world trade with China that occurred in the early 1970s. But China is not alone in growing this wonderful plant; more than 35 other countries grow the *Camellia sinensis* bush from which all true tea comes. Some of the world's finest teas come from Indonesia, Taiwan, Vietnam, Sri Lanka, Nepal, India, Kenya, and Japan. Thanks to the phenomena of geography — weather and topography, especially — each country offers a difference in taste, even when the very same processes are employed.

MANY HANDS BRING YOU TEA
Like all agricultural crops, tea depends upon the gentleness of nature to find a home to grow in, but humans take it from there with careful planting, plucking, processing, and packaging. It takes many hands to bring you a cup of tea; perhaps our first reflection should be gratitude to the hands of the tea farmers and pluckers for the bounty and accessibility of this amazing plant that gives us our daily cup of tea.

Fact and Fiction

Most of the stories about tea's early history are just that — stories. They're amplified with tales of skulduggery, piracy, undiscovered and rediscovered botany, ship races, love, passion, all burnished with the patina of years of retelling. As a result, tea is now the most consumed beverage in the world, after water. In fact, the world consumes 1 billion cups or more of tea per day, making tea the river that runs through family, neighborhood, and country, soothing us during times of sorrow, invigorating us during times of joy.

The story of tea began with its use as a medicine. Tea then became a beverage to keep monks alert, and later it passed down from royalty to the privileged and, finally, to the masses. Today we have come full circle in understanding the beneficial role of tea as a health-giving brew while at the same time learning to appreciate tea's superb qualities as a beverage. May the next 3,000 years of tea history provide increased enjoyment, sharing, and appreciation.

Tea was not only a remedy against drowsiness. It was a way of aiding men to return to their sources, a moment in the rhythm of the day when prince and peasant shared the same thoughts and same happiness while preparing to return to their respective fates.

— Lu Yü, *The Classic of Tea*
(the first Chinese book devoted to tea)

Tea is the beverage of ceremonious peoples, and like the dense monsoon rains, it is both calming and stimulating, encouraging conversation and relaxation . . . Ideas and traditions steep slowly in its steamy transparence.

— Pascal Bruckner, *Parais*

A Short Primer on Tea

No one ever lives long enough to taste each great tea that grows, but, ah — the quest! For the utmost enjoyment, you must respect the leaf and adopt the best ways to buy, store, brew, and serve tea. You must be willing to spend time with tea. In return, tea will give you its many pleasures.

What Is Tea?

All the teas mentioned in this book are true teas, those from the *Camellia sinensis* bush. True teas are not to be confused with herbal "teas," which are actually infusions made with water and the flowers, roots, bark, seeds, or leaves of herbs. Many of those presented here are superior, extra-fine teas available from serious tea merchants and tea blenders. Seek them out for the ultimate drinking pleasures.

If all true teas come from the same botanical plant, why are there so many types, so many flavors? The answer is in how they are processed. Put succinctly, the objective of processing is to take some water out of the fresh leaves and mold the leaves into attractive shapes for the highest-quality brews, or cut the leaves to make each pound of tea go further.

Processing Makes All the Difference

The drying process is called oxidation, and it works much like the process that turns a cut apple or pear brown. For tea, this oxidation, or exposure to air, is intentional. The more completely the leaves are oxidized, the longer they will last. Oxidation also changes the flavor and the aroma; generally (but not always), the more a tea is oxidized, the stronger it tastes. The hows and whys of oxidation are still highly guarded tools of the trade and rarely revealed to outsiders. We must be content to enjoy the results of this combination of art and science.

Choosing Accoutrements

In China and Japan, tea is sipped from tiny 1- to 3-ounce cups, ensuring that the host and guest will take the time required to truly enjoy tea. In Europe and America, we use anything from 5-ounce dinnerware cups to gigantic 12-ounce mugs. When it comes to accoutrements, select vessels that are comfortable to your hand and visually appealing.

Teapots and Cups

Perhaps the most important "teaware" you can have is a good teapot and a few attractive cups. I have tried so very hard not to amass a collection, but cups and pots seem to fall from the sky into my hands, pleading to be filled up with the sweetness of a green tea, a wisp of a white tea, the alluring aroma of an oolong, the stimulation of a smooth black.

I have snow-white thimble cups, tiny Yixing teapots, a jade-and-silver cup from Tibet, a cracked blue-flower and cream teapot I cannot bear to discard, elegant three-legged lusterware cups, museum-caliber glass teapots . . . well, you get the idea.

What am I to do? I opt for the simplest solution: Enjoy each and every one. I use them all for all types of teas, except the Yixing teapots. Because of their special porous clay, I brew the same type of tea in the same Yixing pots each time. (Another reason to add one more pot.)

Getting to Know Tea

What follows is an outline of the general categories of teas. There are more than 10,000 known types of tea processed from more than a dozen varietals of the *Camellia sinensis* plant. The vagaries of weather, altitude, seasons, and other natural factors combined with enormous differences in processing determine the many types. For example, an oolong can be made from Darjeeling, Ceylon, or Taiwan tea; a green can be processed from Japanese, Ceylon, Chinese, or Indian tea.

Green, Yellow, and White Teas

These teas are not oxidized at all but just lightly air- or steam-dried. Only the tiny leaf buds make up white and yellow teas. For greens, the two young, tender leaves from the very top of each tea bush are plucked, then shaped into balls, long spidery twists, or short leaves of elegance and style.

Whites, yellows, and greens are light tasting with a grassy sweetness, yet each is significantly different from the others. Almost all whites, yellows, and greens come from China, although Sri Lanka and India are experimenting with whites and yellows. These two countries, along with Japan and Vietnam, also produce greens.

Oolongs

Oolongs are oxidized on a varied scale, from 2 to 80 percent, creating wildly diverse tastes — yet, remarkably, all have that similar sweet finish and the amazing aroma that is both delicately floral and earthy. The manipulation of oolong leaves is also varied, but the leaves are always quite large. A subcategory of oolongs, pouchongs, are teas that are barely oxidized. They look green, yet have the taste and aroma particular to all oolongs.

Taiwan is the primary producer of oolongs, but China creates many premier examples.

Black Teas

Black tea is 100 percent oxidized and the most frequently drunk tea in the world, in both single-estate and blended forms. Black teas are smooth, rich, and highly aromatic and are made either as a broken or full leaf or as a crushed leaf for more intense flavor.

Nearly all of the tea-producing countries make black teas. Although techniques are quite similar, black teas from different countries do indeed have different tastes.

Pu-erhs

Often called Chinese penicillin, pu-erh is a type of tea you either love or deplore. Its musty smell is a result of intentional aging plus, allegedly, the addition of friendly bacteria for aiding digestion. Pu-erh also cuts cholesterol and helps wean coffee drinkers away from the bean.

Pu-erh, which is made primarily in China, provides a dark, rich, thickish brew that is very satisfying and great to drink before bedtime. It is 100 percent oxidized, and it's usually aged by being buried in the ground in earthen jars for up to 50 years or being processed through sophisticated machinery that shortens the aging process considerably.

Tea Blends

The finest of the teas described above are from single estates or regions. But like all prized items, they may not be plentiful enough to meet demand.

For centuries, tea producers have mixed together different teas to make blends. These blends offer a more rounded taste, benefiting from one tea for body, another for fragrance, and a third (or more) for taste. Many large-scale tea blenders use 60 or more teas from many different countries to achieve their signature flavors, making blending both an art and a science.

Scented and Flavored Teas

Jasmine tea is most often green tea scented with the jasmine flower, although some blenders use a black tea. Earl Grey is a black or green tea flavored with the oil of the bergamot, a citrus fruit, or, in other versions, with petals of lavender. The combinations are endless and always interesting. Make sure that any dried fruit, herbs, flower petals, or food-grade essential oils you use are organic — otherwise you'll drink an unromantic, unhealthy, and foul-tasting version of perfume!

Showplace Teas

For the Chinese or Taiwan mudan, or showplace tea, skilled artisans tie together black or green tea leaves to form the shape of a flower, fruit, or bird's nest. The shapes "blossom" in water and look particularly fanciful in a wineglass. The infusion time is very long, up to 30 minutes — a surefire entertainment for your guests.

How to Brew Tea

Brewing tea requires attention, time, and the best-quality water and tea you can afford. You can't rush tea, nor can you rush pleasure. With just a little patience, the joy of this simple leaf is yours.

Purchase teas in small quantities, and keep them in tightly sealed glass jars, stainless-steel tins, or porcelain canisters; store in a cool, dark cupboard. Use them within several weeks of purchase.

Before brewing, rinse the pots and cups with hot water. Cover with saucers or lids, and set them aside to keep warm while you make tea. Then select a tea to suit your mood or the time of day, or "just because."

Step 1: Measure the Tea

Following the merchant's directions or those on the package, measure out the tea. When in doubt, begin with 2 grams of tea per person or a level teaspoon of tea per 6 ounces (150 ml) of spring water. Putting extra in "for the pot" is a waste of tea and can make the brew too strong.

Step 2: Heat the Water

Generally, the more processed the tea, the hotter the water and the longer the steeping time. Start out with the suggested quantity of leaves and water temperature, and then adjust to taste. The better the quality of the tea, the more infusions you can produce from one serving of leaves.

When selecting water, opt for spring water or high-quality municipal water. Filters for tap water are good, but take care that they do not remove all the good minerals along with the impurities, because natural minerals help greatly to draw out tea's flavor. Avoid distilled and purified waters.

Water temperature is critical. Forget what you've read for years about boiling water; it's rarely required for fine teas, except for the heartiest of black teas or for pu-erhs, which requires boiling water because of their "friendly" bacteria. Generally:

* **For whites,** use water at 175 to 185°F (79 to 85°C). Steep for 30 seconds for the first infusion, 1 minute or longer for the second.
* **For greens,** use water at 185 to 190°F (85 to 88°C). Steep for 30 to 45 seconds for the first infusion, 1 minute or longer for the second.
* **For oolongs,** use water at 185 to 195°F (85 to 90°C). Steep for 1 to 3 minutes for first infusions; second infusions may require 2 to 4 minutes.
* **For blacks,** use water at 195 to 205°F (90 to 96°C). Steep 2 to 5 minutes for first infusions; second infusions may require 3 to 6 minutes.
* **For pu-erhs,** use water at 212°F (100°C; a rolling boil). Steep for 3 to 5 minutes for first infusions; second infusions may require 6 to 8 minutes.

These are, of course, guidelines. Always adjust to suit your taste.

Step 3: Decant

Always pour off all the tea from the freshly brewed leaves at once, using a strainer. Allowing the water to rest on brewed leaves results only in bitter liquor.

If making just a cup of tea, pour all the liquid from the brewing vessel into your cup. When making tea for several people, brew, then decant all the tea into cups. Should there be any leftover tea, decant it into another prewarmed teapot. Rebrew the leaves for a second pot, as desired.

Step 4: Savor

You are now ready to savor your tea. Look at the color of the brew in your cup. Inhale its distinctive fragrance. Sip your tea slowly; really, *really* taste the tea on your tongue. Feel its texture all through your mouth. Close your eyes. Ease yourself back into your chair. Empty your mind.

Welcome to the intoxicating world of tea.

When the water looks to have fish eyes, and the hint of sound, it is at its first stage, and excellent for white or green teas; when it looks like pearls strung together, it is in its second stage, and excellent for oolongs and blacks. If, however, it leaps like ocean's waves, it is boiled out and should not be used.

— Lu Yü, *The Classic of Tea*

spring

sencha in springtime

Spring is like awakening from a restful slumber. Everything is fresh, renewed. A crocus wiggles its way through snow. A litter of puppies arrives, a foal is born. The first of the vegetables emerges. We are reminded that life is a cycle of bounty, to plant, reap, enjoy once again.

Spring is a particularly important time in the growing of tea. The first "plucking" (harvest) occurs between March and April, kind weather permitting, with slight variations from country to country. These first leaves are the tenderest, providing a nearly ephemeral taste in the cup that is different from the flavor of teas from summer or autumn.

Of all the seasonal hallmarks, the spring solstice means the most to me. It is a gentler change of seasons, a slow-moving moon and sun, a time for reflection on the past and on hope for the future.

To think of time — of all that retrospection,
To think of to-day, and the ages continued henceforward.
 . . . Pleasantly and well-suited I walk,
Whither I walk I cannot define, but I know it is good,
The whole universe indicates that it is good,
The past and present indicate that it is good.
How beautiful and perfect are the animals!
How perfect the earth, and the minutest thing upon it!

— Walt Whitman, "To Think of Time"

Create an Atmosphere

Whatever your fitness profile, take a walk among the blossoming wildflowers or a stroll through a public park or garden. Touch a tree, smell a flower, sit among the tall reeds and sweet grasses of a meadow. Take a small journal or sketch pad in which to write or draw. This is "doodle-dawdle" time, to listen, look, and experience the world around you — leisurely, quietly, without any pressure.

Pack a thermos of spring tea, like a refreshing sencha from Japan. Sencha has many different varieties, from the exquisitely delicate to an assertive, tangy, vegetable taste. Add sandwiches of cream cheese garnished with organic peppery nasturtiums; thinly sliced, crisp English cucumber with real sweet butter; or peanut butter and jelly for familiarity and comfort, plus some oatmeal or chocolate-chip cookies, and you're set to rest in your special spot, greeting the beauty of spring.

Question: What is spring?
Growth in everything.

— Gerard Manley Hopkins,
"The May Magnificat"

A Meditation for Spring

Think back upon springs of childhood — the most magnificent April, showers and all, or the sweetest May. What are the blessings of those times that you carry with you now? How have they added to your life? Which ones would you like to repeat? What are the remembered springs with your mate, or children, or best friends? When was the last time you told these beloved how much they mean to you?

When you arrive back home, share a poem or drawing with them, tell them in person how grateful you are to have them in your life this spring and every season.

A new baby is like the beginning of all things — wonder, hope, a dream of possibilities.

— Eda J. LeShan, *The Conspiracy Against Childhood*

welcoming green-tea brunch

Religious and cultural observances of a birth are loving ways to welcome a life to this earth. We can celebrate with a baptism or a naming ceremony, hold a child up to the stars and the moon, gather around a cradle to say "Welcome to our world, little one," incorporating traditional prayers or innovative blessings. A birth is cause to celebrate ourselves . . . and reason to put on the kettle.

Celebrating our cultural traditions or adapting them to create our own ceremonies helps us understand that no matter how different we may appear to one another, the similarities are even greater. No festivity is as powerful or important as the celebration of a newborn child — a person who can unite families or nations. Even in cultures that drink herbal infusions instead of tea (yes, there are some!), the bubbling sound of a kettle signals a time of gathering around the hearth to tell stories and embrace each other in the love of community.

Create an Atmosphere

Make it easy for the baby and the mom, if possible, by celebrating in the family home. Other venues that may work are a friend's home; the family's place of worship; and a public beach, park, or forest. Although the joy of this event is boundless, keep the guest list to a few intimate friends and relatives to mark this momentous occasion in a gentle yet personal way.

Soft, quiet music from guitar, flute, and harp is soothing. Choose green plants or fresh spring flowers and pastel napery — wonderful accents to set a party mood. The most important element is not the decor but the love of people who care about the parents and want to offer blessings to the newborn.

Choose the Tea and Accompaniments

Green signals the birth of the season for the tea plant, so green teas are a logical choice for a birth ceremony. Choose a fresh Gyokuro, Dragonwell, green mudan, or any treasured green. Brew gently and decant into a prewarmed porcelain teapot to serve your guests. Although a lightly brewed cup of green tea has only a modest amount of caffeine, nursing mothers may prefer to skip this beverage.

Your menu depends primarily on the day and time; a Sunday-morning brunch seems ideal. Serve buffet-style, offering foods that are catered or contributed by the guests in a coordinated way. Eggs Benedict with asparagus tips, braided breads and sweet rolls, a berry bowl, and fresh figs and pears with Gorgonzola cheese all make excellent brunch selections.

A Special Blessing for Baby

In addition to, or instead of, traditional cultural or religious blessings, ask guests to jot down their wishes or the one kernel of wisdom they want to pass on to the next generation. Provide pastel pieces of paper and pens, and have guests place these "wishes and wisdoms" in a special basket that the baby's oldest sibling, a grandparent, or another older relative passes around.

Consider sentiments that are touching, humorous, serious, gentle. The parents can later place the wishes and wisdoms in a baby book or special scrapbook, along with photos of the celebration, to show the child how welcomed to this world he or she was (and is!). A Polaroid camera will add a sense of immediacy. Keep distracting flashes and camera activity to a minimum by giving the photography duties to just one sensitive friend.

The desire accomplished is sweet to the soul.
— Psalms 13:19

tea ice cream celebration for graduations & other achievements

I smile at the now-faded photo of 26 five-year-olds in white caps and gowns grinning about their first scholastic accomplishment: graduation from kindergarten. The faces are full of anticipation of first grade and, beyond that, the thrills and challenges of grammar school, middle school, high school, then, if possible, university.

Each graduation or religious milestone, each well-graded term paper — each accomplishment is a miracle of sorts, a genuine achievement along our path from education to the working world.

Whether it's a big box of crayons, a treasured piece of jewelry, or even a first car, an acknowledgment of accomplishments is sweet. Every stage of life should be marked: learning to drive, getting that first job (and all the promotions and raises afterward), learning a new language, or even figuring out how to eliminate that blinking 12:00 on the VCR. However small or large an accomplishment may be, celebrate it with dearest friends and family members, serving the finest teas or tea-flavored foods.

The wise man looks into space and does not regard the small as too little, nor the great as too big; for he knows that there is no limit to dimensions.

— Lao-Tzu (Chinese philosopher)

Choose the Teas and Accompaniments

Children in grade school may not be interested in drinking a cup of tea, but a tea-flavored ice cream is delicious fun at any age. Consider chai- or black currant tea-flavored ice cream. Both are available commercially but are also easy to make at home.

Graduations from middle or high school require more sophisticated fare, like an elegant English afternoon tea with all the accoutrements, fresh-baked scones, tiny decorated petits fours, and, of course, tea sandwiches in various shapes and sizes.

How about a noisy Chinatown dinner with pots of hot oolong? Or pitchers of fruited iced teas served with picnic foods in your own backyard or at the soccer field after a winning season? The possibilities are endless.

A SPECIAL BLESSING FOR THE GRADUATE
When all of your guests have gathered and the tea has been poured, recite this verse as a special blessing:

> May you remember the glory of your triumph today
> Carry its wisdom with you always, pass along
> What you learn to others, sharing, caring, and
> Look back upon your life as a series of sweet passages.

CAMEROON CARAMEL ICE CREAM

Cameroon is an African tea with a naturally sweet finish that marries well with caramelized sugar. This recipe comes from chef and pastry expert Robert Wemischner, creator of the recipes for *Cooking with Tea*.

    ¾ cup sugar
    3 cups heavy cream
    1 cup whole milk
    4 egg yolks
    2 teaspoons Cameroon tea or other black tea of choice

1. In a heavy saucepan, heat the sugar over medium heat without stirring; simply swirl the pan until the sugar melts and turns golden brown. Remove from heat.

2. In another pan, heat the cream and milk until scalded. Carefully add the heated liquid to the caramelized sugar, stirring constantly with a wooden spoon until the mixture is well blended. (It may bubble up vigorously, so be careful.)

3. Place egg yolks in a small heatproof bowl. Remove about 1 cup of the milk-caramel mixture, and add to the eggs to temper (prevent curdling).

4. Add the tea leaves to the remaining milk-caramel mixture and allow to steep for 10 to 15 minutes. Pour this mixture through a fine-mesh sieve, and then return the liquid to the saucepan.

5. Add the egg yolk mixture to the tea mixture and cook over medium heat, stirring constantly with a whisk, until the mixture thickens slightly and the whisk leaves tracks. Do not overcook.

6. Half fill a large bowl with ice cubes and rest a second, smaller bowl on top of the ice. Pour the mixture through a sieve into the top bowl. Chill in the refrigerator until cooled. (Prechilling the mixture gives a better texture with less crystallization.)

7. Freeze in an ice cream machine according to the manufacturer's instructions. When frozen, place ice cream in a container with a tight-fitting lid, and allow it to sit in the freezer for at least 2 hours or overnight, if time permits. This mellows the flavors. Soften slightly before serving.

About 1 quart

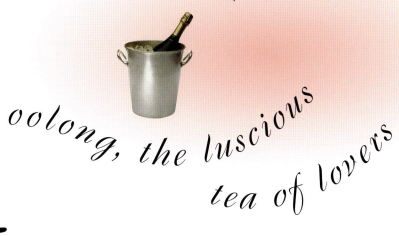

oolong, the luscious tea of lovers

I know a couple who are both mathematicians. While one knits and the other poses math problems, they calculate logarithms and solve the puzzles in their heads. It is their way of relaxing. Another couple reads recipes aloud as if they were poems, tempting each other without the burden of calories, not to mention the labor of shopping and preparation.

How do you make your times alone together special? You could read a mate's choice of poetry, even though it's not yours; do a crossword puzzle together; play chess or another board game; sing arias or show tunes; or just talk about things that really count to you.

Rekindling relationships is important as an ongoing process. Maybe you're saying, "But I don't have time!" It's true that your responsibilities are awesome, but there are always ways to fulfill them and still keep your primary relationship vital. Trade child care with a neighbor or friend; you all deserve the time off. Develop a network of available baby-sitters so you can make a date each week with your mate — and keep it. Use tea as a signal to recall those soft, fun times when you first met, first looked into each other's hearts, first began this part of the journey through life.

If I was going to hug you
it wouldn't be a Hug-Hug/Kiss-Kiss sort
   of hug.
If I was going to hug you
it wouldn't be a show-biz air kiss
slight lean into the void between us.
No, if I was going to hug you
I would step into you . . . slowly,
my hands skiing the firm sand dunes of
   your arms
my palms on your hands,
my fingers circling 'round
the back of your wrists
a gentle stethoscope feeling for . . . the
   pulse of you.
If I was going to hug you
my left arm would seek that
deep impression behind your waist,
climb your vertebrae
memorize each one;
sweep the silky hairs
along your nape.
Together,
my hands would smooth
your furrowed brow
still-soft cheeks
the fullness of your lips.
My face would Eskimo-kiss
the arch of your neck,
my body brush yours . . . hello.

If I was going to hug you.

Create an Atmosphere

As a prelude, take a leisurely stroll through the neighborhood; hold hands; return home to dance to the oldies-but-goodies; feed each other delicacies you both adore; give each other massages with only a whisper of music in the background.

All you need is one room, each other, and time to yourselves. Make it special with fresh flowers, the softest sheets and comforter, and quiet to celebrate each other.

Choose the Tea and Accompaniments

Formosa, Tikwanyin, or another fine oolong — famous for romantic fragrance and rich, satisfying taste — is perfect for this occasion.

If cooking for your mate is something you do with love, by all means make her or his preferred light nibbles. But you'll have more time to enjoy each other if you order an hors d'oeuvre platter from your local gourmet shop to serve with gigantic strawberries, chocolate truffles, and other finger foods.

A Meditation for Lovers

Now that you have taken a walk, danced, fed one another, or made other gestures of courting, this is the moment for absolute silence, to meditate upon each other. The silence accompanying undivided attention to your mate can be a profound aphrodisiac.

In the softly lit room of your choice, sit across from one another. Hold hands; note the strength, the softness. Look into each other's eyes as if for the first time. Gaze upon the mouth of that face you adore. Close your eyes; breathe deeply and fully until your whole body is relaxed and ready to express your affection.

Seal the bliss by preparing a sweet cup of tea for your loved one. Drink it slowly and with pleasure.

summer

The sea is at its best at London, near midnight, when you are within the arms of a capacious chair, before a glowing fire, selecting phases of the voyages you will never take.

— Henry Major Tomlinson, *The Sea and the Jungle*

earl grey comes to a bon voyage party

Ever since I saw Fred Astaire and Ginger Rogers sail off for dancing and romance on the high seas, I've wanted a bon voyage party on a boat. I don't need to go anywhere, mind you — I just want an all-white stateroom where the porter arranges a magnificent floral display, presents me with a huge basket of exotic, out-of-season fruit, and, of course, simultaneously brews me a pot of the most aromatic Earl Grey tea.

I'll play hostess to all the terribly charming, simply divine people who come to send me off in style: the men, resplendent in top hats and tails, and the women, who sweep into the stateroom in their diaphanous silk gowns. Fred will whisk me away to the upper promenade deck to dance the Continental while powder blue feathers from my oh-so-chic boa float up into the air, leaving poor Ginger to pout jealously beside the railing.

Ah, armchair traveling — a fascinating experience — is so economical, but for the more adventurous travel is the way to get outside of our neighborhoods and ourselves. The very act of leaving our home base encourages us to learn more about ourselves and how we cope, to meet new people, to experience new cultures and traditions, and to see more of the world.

Create an Atmosphere

Elegance is the watchword here. Bring out all your dining finery, from silver to candles to fine porcelain. Rent a silver urn for the tea; hire servers dressed in black and white; and request that every guest bring some anecdote, a travel gadget, or a clever idea for packing, overcoming jet lag, or making contacts while traveling.

You'll be amazed to discover who knows someone in Ottawa or Machu Picchu, and meeting these people might even be the highlight of the trip. Probably one of your friends or relatives has visited the traveler's destination and can share tips on where to find the best buys on theater and concert tickets, where the best flea markets are, or how to dress when browsing through bazaars.

Choose the Tea and Accompaniments

Earl Grey could be considered the original "traveler's tea." It was named for that British Earl Grey, who was prime minister of England from 1830 to 1834. He sailed to China, made friends with a highly placed mandarin, and received the first version of this bergamot-scented black tea as a thank-you for his political and economic support.

Share your intriguing traveler's tales with one another over a generous cup of tea and a lavish table of treats, including:

* Trio of blueberry, raspberry, and plain golf-ball-size scones
* Bite-size sandwiches of watercress and cream cheese; heirloom tomatoes and sweet butter; and warmed Brie on toast points
* Vanilla-scented meringues
* Fresh kiwis, cut in half, served with sterling teaspoons to carve out the fruit

I never travel without my diary. One should always have something sensational to read on the train.

—Oscar Wilde, *A Woman of No Importance*

WARMED BRIE ON TOAST POINTS

The marriage of sweet yet tart apricots with rich Brie is ambrosial. Buy the best bread you can find. Microwaves vary, so keep an eye on this! You can also heat the Brie in an oven at about 350°F (176°C), for about 5 minutes.

    2 slices Italian or French white bread, about ¼ inch thick
    3 ounces Brie
    4 dried apricots, finely chopped (optional)

1. Warm Brie slightly in the microwave on medium heat until just melted, about 2 minutes.
2. Toast bread slices in toaster or toaster oven, and then cut each into four triangles (halve each piece, then slice on the diagonal into quarters).
3. Spread warmed Brie on toast points, and serve immediately. Garnish with chopped dried apricots, as desired.

2 servings

He found the longest summer day too short.

— Izaak Walton, *The Compleat Angler*

sun teas for a family reunion

Every year, my aunt Verda's 11 brothers and sisters, their children, and other family members gather for a reunion on the Fourth of July. Several times when I was a teenager, she took me along and introduced me as her niece. It was our little joke that her family was so large, no one realized for several years that I was related not by blood but only through her marriage to my uncle.

Family reunions are wonderful ways to get together, often without the intensity of a holiday to divert our attention from one another. Some families take over entire wings of hotels to combine vacation and reunion; others convene at homes that can accommodate such numbers of people; still others choose community halls for their reunions.

The objectives remain the same whatever the venue: to rekindle the connection that only family can give, introduce the babies, memorialize the dead, and celebrate the living and their passages and accomplishments.

Whether your family is small enough to count on one hand or so huge you need logistical training to track them, keep in touch. No matter how near or far they are, make the effort this year to say, "Let's get together for a family reunion."

In a summer season when soft was the sun . . .
— William Langland, "Piers Plowman"

Create an Atmosphere

What could be more comfortable or easier than a summertime reunion picnic in a park? Have all guests bring photos of themselves or of recent special events. Drape a few white sheets on a clothesline strung between two trees, and use them as a bulletin board for your photos and news. Just pass out straight pins or tape, and *voilà!* a casual but fun glimpse of the past years.

With desktop publishing so accessible these days, you'll no doubt be able to find a few relatives willing to put the memorabilia into a book. Or create your own family Web site! At the very least, print a complete address book for everyone to take away from the reunion as a way to keep in touch.

Choose the Tea and Accompaniments

One of the quirks in life in Phoenix is the chorus line of fat, clear-glass jars that seem to appear like magic on the sidewalks every morning. They begin as jars of tea bags dancing in clear water. By noontime the sun has drawn out the nectar of the tea leaves, and one by one the jars are brought into the houses for drinking the rest of the day.

Any tea will do, but greens and blacks are best, and Nilgiri blacks are exceptional for their lack of cloudiness and their ability to be brewed at length, by sun or heated water, without bitterness. Use 8 to 10 teabags or 6 to 8 teaspoons of loose tea per gallon. Iced sun teas taste even better with plenty of sliced peaches, nectarines, or other summer fruit splashing in the glass.

The cuisine your family favors, from Thai to African to Latin American to any point in between, should be part of the menu. Look for cookbooks in bookstores or libraries that best reflect your heritage or that focus on reunion. When in doubt, bring out American picnic fare and gallons of sun tea!

CHRIS SITTIG'S POTATO-BEET SALAD

My friend Chris always packs this delicious potato salad for outings to the beach. The beets and capers add a sweet, salty surprise to familiar potatoes.

2 large Yukon gold or white potatoes
1 bunch yellow or red beets, about 4 large or 6 medium
1 tablespoon capers, or to taste
   Salt and pepper
   Mayonnaise to blend, about 2 tablespoons

1. Boil potatoes and beets just until tender but not mushy. Cool in cold water.
2. Peel off potato and beet skins. Slice the potatoes and beets into hefty chunks and place in a large bowl.
3. Add the capers, a dash of salt and pepper, and enough mayonnaise to blend thoroughly. Chill until ready to serve.

4 ample servings

SHARING A PRAYER

Many families are connected further by a shared religion from which you can select prayers for gatherings. This is the best time for the youngest school-age children to demonstrate their beginning education into your culture. What is more awesome than seeing a small child light religious candles or sing a hymn alone or accompanied by your eldest relative? Ask teenagers to write a meditation or blessing incorporating dance, poetry, and song, or even a little play that honors your family's religious and cultural traditions. They'll love finding this channel for their energy, and their creativity will astonish.

darjeeling for the darlings: an engagement party

O h, love. To meet someone so special you want to spend the rest of your life with him or her is perhaps our most romantic notion. Despite the shocking statistics about divorce, hope continues as couples marry in record numbers, many of them in elaborate festivities celebrating a union of souls.

The engagement party is a charming tradition both to announce the impending marriage and to introduce close friends and family of the prospective bridegroom to those of the prospective bride. This is a time to share family anecdotes and to bask in the love and support of one another. When the actual wedding takes place, the audience comprises not strangers but familiar faces. As they see one another at holidays and special occasions in the years to come, they will have the opportunity to be more than just acquaintances — they can become friends.

Create an Atmosphere

Make the location one that is special, warm, and inviting for all. A family home is the most intimate place to announce an engagement, but a dinner party at a local restaurant is equally gracious.

Pretty is the decoration style of choice. If you're entertaining at home, bring out the family silver, fine tablecloths, and dinnerware. Fresh flowers, pastel ribbons, and a light touch of lace all will be charming accents.

Favors are terrific tokens of appreciation from the newly engaged couple to their guests. Why not wrap some scented teas, like vanilla, in pieces of lace or satin and tie with colorful ribbon? Attach a little card that says, "It is a blessing to have you share our special day," "We're so happy you are a part of our lives," or those two timeless words — "Thank you"!

Choose the Tea and Accompaniments

What tea should you serve? Darjeeling, of course, the champagne of teas!

The specialty of the house is the obvious choice when hosting the party at a restaurant, and a potluck at home would be a marvelous way to introduce each family's specialties. Whether it's Aunt Diane's Parmesan crackers or salmon-pecan log or Grandma's peasant eggplant caviar, sharing with each other the favorite foods of two families is a loving tribute and a great way to reflect everyone's new connection to the happy couple.

Tell Secrets!

Every happy couple has one "secret" that accounts for its successful union. Ask those with the longest marriages or those who are deemed unique by everyone to share their secrets of happiness. Afterward, a father, special aunt, or brother from each family can offer a toast or blessing for a loving life together, and a thank-you to the couple for joining these two families.

HAPPILY MARRIED

Who could imagine wedding plans exploding
the good sense of this practical family; her father
refused to wear his new Sunday suit, her niece
wanted to somersault down the aisle, her mother
invited everyone she knew to 'just drop by,' so Mary said,
'George, we're eloping. Tonight. Let's take the 6:58 to Reno;
we'll be there by 9, married by 11, start tomorrow as Mr. and Mrs.'
Best decision they ever made.
Oh, she did love that man;
fifty-three years seemed like fifty-three minutes. She closes her eyes, rests
in the wing chair so like his embrace. She dreams. Hums.
On the bureau, his keys, change, frayed wallet holding
that perennial token of his love, the fragile, near transparent blue ticket
     stub from that starlit bus trip long ago.

fall

True silence is the rest of the mind; and it is to the spirit what sleep is to the body, nourishment and refreshment.

— William Penn, "Advice to His Children"

after-school kids tea

Have you seen the homework of children these days? It's very humbling to realize how much they need to learn. I'm always shocked; even geography, the very countries that make up our world, involves new names, borders, even languages.

Perhaps my parents were just as amazed at the "new" things I had to learn, but some things never do change: First and foremost, kids need a break from their school days to play, relax, and have fun with friends. And they need to learn that being quiet and resting are very good things to do. These regenerative acts are important keys to successful living in adulthood.

After school is a perfect time for tea, sipped slowly as tales of the day are revealed. The sounds of children's voices describing recess excitement, the astonishment gleaned from learning something new, the funny, the odd, all the images that capture your child: These are what afternoon tea time is all about.

Although "When I was your age" may elicit moans, children really do love stories about where you grew up, what feelings you had about school and playmates, how you learned to handle the sometimes confusing passages from child to young adult, and, of course, all the jokes and riddles you still remember!

Create an Atmosphere

What everyone needs after a long day is time to "decompress." The kitchen is the ideal place, especially during fall and winter when it can be bitterly cold outside. The warmth from the stove is a welcome relief. Bring out your child's favorite mug or glass for this intimate time together.

Choose the Tea and Accompaniments

The best tea for this event is a hearty black Assam. Serve 1 part tea with 3 parts hot milk and a teaspoon of sugar or honey. It makes the kids feel like grown-ups to taste tea, but they won't get the punch of caffeine. Decaffeinated tea is an alternative.

Whether you are with your children when they come home or you have a sitter, help them make good food choices. If you have the luxury of time and the right schedule, you can make some dishes in advance and reheat them at teatime. Your children can even join you in baking cookies. Homemade always tastes the best, but the premixed varieties are great time-savers; you need only pop some cookie dough into the oven and wait 10 minutes for the sweet smell of cookies to waft through the kitchen.

For a healthy snack menu, try assorted nuts and dried fruits, baked apples, and pumpkin cookies.

A MEDITATION FOR CHILDREN

Encourage your children to take time out every day to be quiet, without the assault of a noisy television, a CD player, or even the friendly noises of playmates. Help your children create their own prayers or blessings of gratitude by suggesting how, for example, they can be thankful for school and learning itself. Let them know that some children do not have free libraries, free public schooling, or free parks available to them.

Your children can even learn how to use meditation at school. Suggest they seek out a corner during recess or lunchtime, or use their study hour for quiet contemplation and rest.

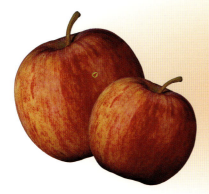

Listen! the wind is rising,
and the air is wild with leaves,
We have had our summer evenings,
now for October eves!

— Humbert Wolfe, "Autumn"

KID-LOVIN' BAKED APPLES

The smell of baked apples always means fall, brilliant-colored foliage, and mittens for the oncoming colder weather. These apples are delicious for breakfast, too! Asian pears, which taste like delicate apples with a hint of the sweetness of Bosc pears, also work well.

2 large Rome or Fuji apples
2 heaping tablespoons raisins
½ teaspoon ground cinnamon
2 tablespoons light brown sugar
1 tablespoon lemon zest

1. Preheat oven to 350°F (176°C). Grease a small loaf pan.
2. Core apples and use a knife to make a shallow, X-shaped slit over the top hole to prevent the skin from bursting. Place apples snugly in the pan and stuff raisins, cinnamon, and brown sugar into the cavities. Sprinkle with the lemon zest.
3. Pour about a half inch of water into the bottom of the pan. Bake for 30 to 40 minutes, until the juice runs out when the apples are pierced with a knife.
4. Cool slightly. Serve in a bowl with a bit of warm milk, or plain, with any remaining apple-soaked water.

2 servings

Peace be to this house.
— Luke 10:5

a housewarming with keemun & fruited iced teas

The first apartment, a weekend retreat, the retirement home — settling into a new nest is always an accomplishment to celebrate. One of the most intriguing housewarming parties I ever attended was also the most heartfelt and dearest. Parents came, and friends arrived, from each aspect of the hostess's professional and personal lives. Most of us did not know one another, but we all shared one thing: a love for our mutual friend.

The apartment was simple, clean, and waiting for love to warm it up. All the guests brought gifts reflecting house blessings from their personal cultures or religions. In came braided egg bread and salt, brooms to sweep away bad vibes or ghosts, stones from all corners of the earth to be placed in the four corners of the apartment, prayers, and songs of beauty and sweetness. Each guest wrote, then recited a personal blessing, and none was a repeat: love, peace, quiet, safety, and a new boyfriend, but that's another story . . .

The written blessings are now scattered on my friend's personal altar of special things: Some of these things are religious, others are weird or whimsical, and many are traditional, like candles, incense, photographs, poetry.

Create an Atmosphere

Sunday brunch is a great time for a housewarming; people are away from the demands of the workplace, ready to relax and share their best wishes for the new homeowner. Weather and space can steer guests outside to the patio or yard, or inside into the new kitchen and living room.

Although much of the decor will be created by prayer offerings, gifts, and tokens from your guests, set the tone for this special day with fresh flowers, your best china and silver, and the finest cloth napkins.

Choose the Tea and Accompaniments

A hot China black tea, like Keemun (Qiman), is easily prepared in a rented samovar and served in porcelain cups. For iced tea, brew a black tea, then chill for a few hours. Prior to serving, add a cup of freshly cut fruit of the season — oranges, strawberries, pineapples, peaches, apples — for each quart of tea; pour into chilled glasses. If you want to add ice cubes, freeze apple or orange juice in an ice-cube tray for extra flavor.

French toast, pancakes, egg dishes, sweet breads and rolls, lots of fresh fruit — all are perfect buffet brunch fare for a housewarming.

'Mid pleasures and palaces though we may roam,
Be it ever so humble, there's no place like home.
— John Howard Payne, from *Clari; or, The Maid of Milan*

Offering Blessings and Good Cheer

You might like to have one person or a group recite this verse:

> May you be happy, comfortable, safe,
> May your door be always open to friends,
> May your kettle always be singing its welcome
> To you, and all whom you so dearly love.

   You can easily create a shrine to memorialize this day. Create your own altar, as did my friend, or simply collect a group of your special things. Arrange a few of your dearest mementos — those things that call to you and connect you to your deepest self — on a small painted stepladder, windowsill, bookshelf, cloth-draped corner table, any place you have constantly in view.

   After eating delicious food, making new acquaintances, and sharing so many housewarming traditions, my friend passed out colorful three-by-five-inch cards inked with her name, new address, and new telephone number and with a tea bag taped on top. We could all keep in touch and think of this day when we sipped the tea at home. When we left we did not leave an apartment, we left a *home.*

comforting ceylon break at work

Coffee break: That pause every few hours during a conventional workday is a perk for many but is too often ignored because of the demands on your time and attention.

As delicious as good coffee is, a well-made cup hardly finds its way into most mugs in today's convenience-oriented culture. Coffee carafes are kept too long on the burner or allowed to go cold. And coffee's caffeine is overstimulating, leading to a letdown in energy just when you need the boost the most.

While coffee bars generally offer better-tasting coffee, the three- to five-dollar price is considerably more than the most expensive cup of the rarest tea found anywhere in the world, and hardly as exquisite as, say, a Dragonwell, a Makaibari Darjeeling, or a rich Keemun (Qiman).

Tea, ah, tea is what a break from work should be all about. Tea is both energizing and calming to drink. It has considerably less caffeine than coffee per cup, and the type of caffeine is actually assimilated into the body more slowly, more healthfully. Best of all, you can easily make one cup at a time without sacrificing taste.

Wherever you work, or whatever the schedule is, take at least one break each day. You'll perform better, you'll feel better, and you might even influence die-hard coffee drinkers to take a well-deserved, real break . . . with tea.

Create an Atmosphere

At the office, tea drinking can be as simple or as elaborate as space allows. Not every shop, office, and work site has kitchen facilities, but you can still enjoy your tea wherever you are. Yes, even at your desk or counter. If you work outdoors, take advantage of a tree's shade or a sunny spot to sit in. The important thing is to find a corner of quiet, beauty, and calm, where you can sip your tea in peace.

Choose the Tea and Accompaniments

Sri Lanka (formerly Ceylon) has an incredible array of fine teas. Because Ceylons are crisp, clean, and brisk-tasting, they're ideal for a tea break at work. You'll find Ceylon greens, many of them organic, as well as refreshing blacks from crushed leaves and the finest golden-tipped full-leaf styles that are as beautiful to see as they are delicious to drink.

Fill a thermos with hot water, take along some tea bags or a tin of loose-leaf tea, a filter, and a teacup, and you're ready to make tea. What to do with the infused leaves or spent bag? Put them in a plastic bag or wrap in paper and discard, or scatter leaves and leftover liquor on plants at work, inside or out.

Along with your tea, try pick-me-up foods that will give you energy:

* Plain yogurt with fresh fruit you mix in yourself
* A handful of raw cashews mixed with raisins
* A cold, crisp apple
* Rice cakes with peanut butter

Direct your mind inward, and you'll find
A thousand regions of your mind
Yet undiscovered. Travel them . . .
— Henry David Thoreau, "Conclusion" from *Walden*

A Meditation for the Work Day

Get up and walk outside if you're indoors all day; if you're outdoors all day, step inside for a while. Roll your shoulders, stretch your body as much as possible. Close your eyes. Think of all that you have to be grateful for in your work; remember all your past accomplishments. Think of those you love. Sip your hot, refreshing Ceylon tea. Let its warmth comfort you. Be still.

Open your eyes. You'll discover you can continue your day alert and ready to tackle anything because you've enjoyed 10 minutes of respite, with the blessings of a cup of tea.

ON A DAY MADE NEW

On this new autumn morning, we are thankful to be in good health at the sunrise; may we be in good health when the sun sets, and when it rises on the morrow.

irish breakfast on a rainy morning

Whaat can alter our moods more profoundly than the weather? The sound of rain, in particular, is so musical, with a cadence all its own that can lull you into a peaceful state. Let's consider a rainy morning in the autumn for our Irish breakfast. Look out through the rain-draped window and allow the rain to comfort, calm, and soothe you.

Listen for the changes in the sounds of the rain; is it coming down more slowly or faster? Is there thunder or lightning? When we welcome each type of weather, we bring blessings to ourselves. What are the blessings of rain for you? Granted, rain is vital to growing a beautiful vegetable garden, replenishing dry soil, making your part of the world more lushly green. But what are the other benefits? Does it make you appreciate a sunny, warm day all the more? Does it make the cold whiteness of winter seem far away? Does it mean that your springtime flowers will be even more colorful, more fragrant when their time comes?

Choose the Tea and Accompaniments

The implied chill of the rain means your choice of tea this morning should be a hearty black. Make it a vibrant Irish breakfast blend of rich India Assam, softened by a fruity China Keemun (Qiman) and the brightness and color of a wonderful Kenya from Africa. You need some energy for the rest of a day like this, so add a little milk and a teaspoon of sugar to make this a nourishing and refreshing morning brew.

The people of Ireland consume more tea per capita than any other group. They know what it takes to sustain them on the many cold, rainy days in the rocky hills around their villages. Drunk all day long, the classic Irish blend caresses from head to toe. Take a sip of your tea. Feel the hot, milky fluid wend its way down, warming every inch of you.

Have another cup of tea, perhaps with a slice of fresh Irish soda bread or a piece of toast with marmalade. Taking 10 minutes to listen to the rain and enjoy the view while sipping your tea can give you enough energy to live today in a fuller, more bountiful way.

CONTEMPLATE YOUR BLESSINGS

What are some of the blessings of your life? Isn't it wonderful that you have the ability to jog, or the love of a family, or the stimulation of a career, or just the opportunity to see, hear, even smell the rain? What other blessings can you think of?

IRISH BREAKFAST SODA BREAD

The variations on this classic are almost infinite. The buttermilk adds a moistness and tenderness not always found in this sturdy bread.

1	teaspoon baking soda
3	teaspoons baking powder
1	scant teaspoon salt
4	cups flour (preferably a blend of white and whole wheat)
½	teaspoon ground cinnamon
1	cup raisins or currants
1¾	cups buttermilk
1	large egg

1. Preheat oven to 375°F (176°C). Grease two 8-inch round cake pans.
2. In a large bowl, sift together all dry ingredients. Add the raisins or currants.
3. In a separate bowl, beat the buttermilk and egg. Stir the buttermilk mixture into the dry ingredients until you have a smooth batter.
4. Lightly flour a board. Knead the batter on the floured board until smooth.
5. Cut the dough into two parts and form each into a flat round. Place each round in a pan, pressing right up to the edges of the pan. With a knife, make a deep, ½-inch X to divide each round into four wedges; do not cut all the way through. Bake for about 35 minutes, or until lightly browned on the top.
6. Cool just slightly, cut, and serve with marmalade or butter. Leftovers are great toasted and buttered.

8 servings

winter

I am grown peaceful as old age tonight.
— Robert Browning, "Andrea del Sarto"

Delicate whites for a friend in need

Share a cup of tea with someone who may not get out often due to illness, age, injury, or economic or social restrictions. A simple tea celebration can be a very special event to someone in need, and there is always someone more in need than we are. Reaching out to the needy shouldn't be just a thing to do during the holidays. Need knows no calendar, no geographical boundary, no age limit. If all you can do is offer a package of tea, you've done much to bring comfort.

Talk to your grocers or tea merchants; perhaps they have teas they can donate that you can deliver to those in need. If you like to work one-on-one, consider providing the various ingredients of a tea meal to a local convalescent facility or preparing tea for a different small group every month. Or take a few teenagers from the area girls' club out to a local hotel tea every season or, better yet, teach them how to make tea so they can enjoy this experience all through their lives.

The joy of knowing that someone has a cup of hot, soothing tea will warm your heart as it warms the body of the needy one. The gift of some tea and your cheer would be so welcome to all.

Create an Atmosphere

More and more hospitals and long-term-care facilities are tuning into the benefits of decorating with uplifting paintings and sculptures, eschewing the archaic "seasick" green for pleasant-colored walls and trying to bring a little charm into what is, after all, a serious place for health, rehabilitation, or care of the elderly.

You can add a little liveliness to the room of an ill or elderly person or to a shelter by arranging for flowers to be delivered every week. Most florists simply throw out those flowers that don't sell within one day and buy fresh every morning. With careful pruning and clever arranging, these "day-old" flowers can brighten the lives of those who really need the color and fragrance to lift their spirits.

Choose the Tea

In China, white teas are popular among the elderly. These teas have a sweet, delicate taste, with barely a trace of caffeine, and are gentle to the stomach. These qualities have made them very popular among those who are ill or seeking lower-caffeine drinks, as well as those who simply love an ephemeral tea. Silver Needle is the best known and most readily available, but more and more white teas are imported each spring.

Do not the most moving moments of our lives find us all without words?

— Marcel Marceau, from a *Reader's Digest* interview

A Meditation for a Friend

Living teaches a lot of things, and one thing I know: Never wait to say thank you or I love you.

Depending upon the seriousness of the illness or need, leave a few moments during your visit to tell the person how much he or she means to you, has taught you, and has touched you. Offer a concrete wish for the future. We carry these thoughts so often in our hearts, but imagine the joy they give when expressed in person!

If the person is able to give one, ask him or her for a blessing. Even if your friend's energy level only allows a squeeze of your hand, this benediction will stay in your heart wherever you go.

Caretakers need relief, too. Offer to care for their patients so they can have some quiet time for tea and rest.

The holiest of all holidays are those
Kept by ourselves in silence and apart;
The secret anniversaries of the heart.

— Henry Wadsworth Longfellow, "Holidays"

holiday salon with tea punches & cocktails

Looking for something different to acknowledge the holiday season? Why not a Holiday Salon to celebrate friendship? It is a delightful surprise to discover that a coworker has sung in the Civic Light Opera, that a fellow choir member harbors secret tango talent, or that your blustery boss writes lyric poetry. Everyone is part ham — this is the evening to express it! Create your own intimate night of music, dance, poetry, and story-telling. Ask that all performers choose material that celebrates the joy of friendship among people and animals or any thing, place, or time that is a friend to them.

This is a particularly welcome way to celebrate the holidays when you're away from your own family and its traditions. Now, you can start a tradition of your own and embrace the talents and joys of new and old friends.

Those who insist they have no talent to perform must be requested to shout "Brava! Bravo!" at every opportune moment. Or ask them each to tell the group, in their own words, what friendship means to them, or to relate how wonderful their best friend is. (Be mushy or silly; you know your own friends!)

Create an Atmosphere

Wintertime parties almost demand festive buffets, and your Holiday Salon is no exception. Around the room, place bowls full of apples and oranges, roasted chestnuts, and freshly popped popcorn (on the stove, now — no microwave!).

Get lots of pillows for the audience to recline on, and decorate all around with gloriously huge ribbons. The wildest paper plates and napkins you can find are a must. (Friends don't let friends get burdened with dish washing on a holiday!)

Create kibitz corners where people can talk between performances, and let the evening glide on.

Choose the Tea and Accompaniments

A tea punch is a delicious variation on fruit punch and a snap to make. Brew up black tea (decaf works well) and add 1 teaspoon prepared mulling spices or the following for each quart of tea you make: 1 whole cinnamon stick, 1 teaspoon ground allspice, 1 orange (sliced, rinds on). Serve hot or cold. If serving cold, add ice cubes made with orange juice — they add color and flavor and won't dilute the flavor of the tea.

Consider a cup of really great Darjeeling oolong or remarkable Uva or Dimbulla. Each tastes wonderful with a chaser of Irish whiskey. This is the pièce de résistance for hosts to enjoy while cleaning up and talking about the guests and how great the party was!

For your menu, select platters of crudités and dips, steamed squash, tubs of steamed crabs (they're messy, but so much fun!), your traditional holiday foods, and Boffo Brownies.

A HOLIDAY MEDITATION

At the end of the evening, light a few candles in the house, and recite a prayer of thanksgiving for the camaraderie and blessing of friendship, or ask a few friends to recite a special blessing for all the talent in the room, both the engaging performers and the appreciative audience. As guests leave, hand each of them your gift of a small votive holder and candle, tied with a colorful ribbon to remind them they are all vital links in the friendship chain during the holidays and all year long.

BOFFO BROWNIES

Everyone loves brownies, so share this delectable recipe with your guests.

1	level cup all-purpose flour
1	teaspoon baking powder
½	cup unsalted sweet butter, melted and cooled
12	tablespoons dark baking cocoa or 12 ounces of chocolate chips
4	large eggs
2	cups sugar
½	teaspoon salt (or less, to taste)
2	teaspoons pure natural vanilla
1	cup chopped pecans or walnuts

1. Preheat oven to 325°F (176°C). Grease a 9-inch-square pan and set aside.
2. In a bowl, combine the flour with the baking powder.
3. In a separate bowl, mix cooled melted butter with the cocoa and blend until incorporated. Add the eggs and blend well. Add the sugar, salt, and vanilla, and whisk or beat until smooth. Add the nuts and the flour mixture, and stir gently.
4. Pour the batter evenly into the pan, smoothing the top with a rubber spatula. Bake about 30 minutes, testing near the edges of the pan with a tooth-pick; the toothpick will come out clean when the brownies are done.
5. Cool completely. Cut into squares, and serve.

10 to 12 large brownies

cups of kenya for guys' night out & calming chai for gals' night in

You love your family, adore your job, enjoy your day-to-day life. Yet everyone, male and female, needs to spend time away from typical duties, even for just an evening. A warming, soothing cup of tea is just the ticket to relaxation and enjoyment with friends.

A lot of men and women would drink good tea if only it were available. If your group of friends appreciates fine teas, why not have a coed night out at a local tea shop? Ask the owner to create a tea-sampler evening and a question-and-answer session so that everyone can learn more about his or her favorite topic. You'll discover a whole range of choices and alternative ways to brew teas, and you'll learn, in detail, what has only been touched upon in the early chapters of this book.

Remember that tea accoutrements are more than a round teapot, a hand-painted porcelain cup, and silver equipage. Your tea shop experience will introduce you to the celadon porcelain of Korea, the blue-and-white teacups and heirloom wood tea caddies of Japan, exquisite Chinese Yixing ware, and Taiwanese *gung fu* sets — just for a tempting beginning.

for the guys

Create an Atmosphere

Book clubs are sprouting up everywhere; they open up communication you never thought possible. When people discuss ideas, reactions to characters, and philosophy or moral lessons gleaned from books, they reveal sides of themselves you may never have seen before in your usual experiences at work, in the neighborhood, or even within a family. Most libraries have staff picks for suggested reading, or ask your librarian to recommend a few titles, perhaps off the best-seller list, for your group.

Choose the Tea and Accompaniments

For a guys' night out at a friend's home, take along your own tea. Brew a Kenya or another choice at home and keep it hot in a few insulated pots. Ask the host to provide milk and sugar for those who want them. Industrial-size tea bags sold at grocery stores make large quantities of iced teas easy: Put the bag in a large pot of hot water and brew to the strength desired, then chill until ready to serve. That's it!

Make it easy for everyone: Opt for sandwiches, pasta salads, and a great cake. Or call for pizza. In fact, a pizza parlor (with your own freshly made tea) would be a really fun place to have your "guys' night out."

Friendship is a sheltering tree.
— Samuel T. Coleridge, "Youth and Age"

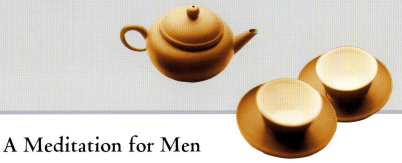

A Meditation for Men

Friendship among men is a special bond and one that a spouse or a business partner cannot always understand. Many men have friends they've known since grade school, or college, or the armed services. Some keep in touch through reunions, others by e-mail, snail-mail, the telephone. Others, because they live so close, are united through hobbies, fraternal organizations, political clubs, sporting events, or a regular guys' night out like this one. Have fun while staying close enough to talk to friends about the things that matter to the soul. Discuss books, jobs, plans for the future — or simply reminisce about good times with friends.

for the gals

Create an Atmosphere

You're never too old for a slumber party. Bring a comfy pillow and blanket, wear your flannel pajamas, and you're ready! This is a great time to try new perfumes, nail polish, or makeup ideas (you can even invite a makeup artist or manicurist for "entertainment"), and you know there will be no gaps in the conversation. This is such a fun way for women to totally relax. As a bonus, consider hiring a massage therapist to give mini-massages to feet, shoulders, and other tension spots. Each person gets 15 minutes of bliss.

A MEDITATION FOR FRIENDS

Instead of counting sheep tonight before sleep, count all your friends and all the blessings they bring to your life. Who makes you laugh? Who shares your tears? Who can you rely on in a pinch? Who will take care of your children or pets with love if you need to be away? Who will take care of your job or business? Whose advice do you trust? Who has stuck by you through thick and thin?

Counting your blessings is a meditation for any night of the year; you're sure to fall asleep before you remember them all.

Choose the Tea and Accompaniments

Call for Chinese food; you've got too much to talk about to spend time cooking!

Iced teas are great with any take-out food, but when (and if) you finally calm down enough to actually go to sleep, brew up hot chai with milk and sugar. Sweet dreams will be yours.

The sweet-spicy richness of a masala chai, the everyday drink of Sikkim and northern India, is a delicious drink at any time of the day. A recipe for masala chai is always just a blueprint, a guideline for adding a little more spice here or choosing a little less there.

MY FAVORITE CHAI

This recipe is from my book *Chai: The Spice Tea of India* (Storey Books, 1999). Experiment with spices and types of teas to see what you enjoy.

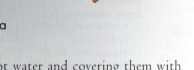

1½	cups water
8	green cardamom pods, crushed
6	whole black peppercorns
2	slices fresh gingerroot, peeled and diced
1	stick cinnamon, 2 inches long
2	whole cloves
⅔	cup whole milk or soy milk
4	teaspoons sugar
3	teaspoons loose-leaf black Assam tea

1. Warm two teacups by filling them with hot water and covering them with their saucers. Set aside.
2. In a saucepan, bring the water and spices to the boil. Reduce heat to low and simmer for about 6 minutes.
3. Add the milk and sugar, and heat to almost boiling. Add the tea leaves and turn off the heat. Let the tea infuse for 3 minutes, or longer, to taste.
4. Strain into cups and serve.

2 servings